VOICES OF REASON

VOICES OF REASON

CALMING THE CONFLICTS IN POLITICAL DISCUSSIONS

BILL ENTZMINGER, PH.D.

To order additional copies of this book, contact:
Xlibris
844-714-8691
www.Xlibris.com
Orders@Xlibris.com
850766

CONTENTS

Dedication

To J. Thad and Bernice Hilton Entzminger, who were devoted to impacting lives by living the gospel they embraced. Dad first exposed me to public political debates, had insights that surpassed that of other adults, yet remained firm in the belief that partisan politics had no place in his pulpit ministry.

Acknowledgements

Thanks to J.T. Entzminger for formatting assistance and moving the book from manuscript to publication, and for providing constant IT work and computer rescue. And to Jared Entzminger for reliable computer advice.

Introduction

The political warfare originating in Washington DC and reverberating throughout the nation has been the most pervasive, headline grabbing news of the last few years in the United States. Most recently, the economy has brought about the strongest debates, but all those circle back to the political issues. For students, government and political science are among the most tedious and, not incidentally, least understood courses they take. So we have a nation of people who found the study of government boring, and yet the reality of what government is doing anything but.

The intent here is to give an easily grasped, common sense, nonpartisan description of the distribution of power within a government, and the belief systems that the different groups embrace. It is through the actions of partisan politics, which are always present when a variety of ideas do battle in the public arena, that real-world outcomes evolve.

The focus here will be the specifics of government as it functions, and has functioned historically, in the United States. This will also be contrasted with the way other governments are structured and function throughout the rest of the world and the directions in which they're very dynamically evolving.

The dual purpose of this writing is to increase knowledge and understanding and thereby, hopefully, inject a much-needed increase in sanity into the current stormy political process.

CHAPTER ONE

WHAT DO THESE TERMS REALLY MEAN, ANYWAY?

Conservative and *liberal* were on the short list of the most searched words on Merriam-Webster.com in 2012. We hear politically laden terms every day: conservative, liberal, reactionary, radical, socialist, democratic, republican, communist, anarchist, and terrorist. A political party will appear to be either conservative or liberal as will politicians, economists, journalists, and media outlets. Each term may be embraced with pride by different people, and each term used as a scornful label against opponents. We may also hear the terms *left wing* and *right wing*. Are these just different labels for liberal and conservative? And then we encounter the term radical being used both ways, as in radical right or radical left, generally as an accusation. Many people use these terms regularly, quite certain they know what they mean. When listeners hear the terms used, they assume they know what the speaker means.

To say someone is a conservative suggests possible things

about that person but of necessity leaves a great deal of material unsaid. This leaves the hearer with the job of filling in for himself all the rest of the missing information. This is called assuming, which could be accurate and frequently is inaccurate. In the current political arena in the United States, conservatives are generally thought to be people who are Republicans, support reducing taxation, oppose expansion of government, oppose gun control laws, oppose abortion, support an expanded military, oppose same-sex marriage, emphasize states' rights and a more limited central government, support petroleum drilling and pipeline construction over environmental concerns and insist on a tough illegal immigration enforcement.

Liberals are generally thought to be people who are Democrats and embrace opposing positions on each of these issues. It's well to keep in mind that there are many conservatives who break ranks on some of these issues and, at least privately, embrace liberal positions. This is equally true of liberals. This is well illustrated by the fact that the voting records of every lawmaker in Washington are scored on what percentage of the time he or she votes the conservative position or votes the liberal position. Most lawmakers do not score 100 percent on either one. This probably, as much as anything, indicates that real life is complex. Most bills include items that are pleasing and items that are displeasing to each lawmaker. However close people may be, if everyone has a functioning brain, there will be differences in opinions.

We all need to clump people, cars, the weather, food or animals into classifications in order to draw comparisons and make decisions. To simply say you talked to a person is a classification label since it implies that you could have been talking to a cat if you so chose. Further, you can classify people as being male or female, old or young, tall or short, or blonde, brunette, or redhead. When you use any of these labels you're only reporting one aspect of a person and leaving out an enormous mass of detail that could also be stated about that person. So having categories with labels is essential to understanding your world. Yet any classification throws away a lot of useful information that cannot be included merely by giving a label, however accurate the label may be.

For most of the classifications in life, a twofold breakdown does not give enough information. To say someone is a male or female is a twofold breakdown that we use daily. If, however, you say someone is either old or young, the listener probably doesn't have enough information. If a thirteen-year-old says someone is old, you don't know if he means an older teen, someone old enough to be his parent, or a senior citizen, which might be important information to have. So, too, the terms conservative and liberal leave us wanting more information.

When some conservatives feel that most other conservatives are not nearly conservative enough, think that the larger group has already moved too far in the liberal direction and that there is a need to return to an earlier time when conservatives were much more conservative, these people are referred to as *reactionaries*. When some liberals feel a great impatience with the great mass of fellow liberals moving far too slowly in changing society and insist on a dramatically increased speed of change in society, or when they embrace positions that are far too liberal for most other liberals, these people are referred to as *radicals*. Therefore, it seems that a fourfold classification remains simple to understand yet has much more utilitarian value than the twofold classification.

Conservatives are frequently referred to as being on the right, while liberals are referred to as being on the left. Reactionaries are then seen as the extreme right and radicals are seen as the extreme left. Most modern western societies are composed primarily of a left and right dealing with each other and making most decisions. When debate heats up and emotion replaces reason, anyone on the right may be referred to by the left as being right wing or extreme right. At such time, those on the right will likely refer to anyone on the left as being the radical left or extreme left. These terms cease being logical terms and become emotional accusations, failing to give useful information about either side. This is somewhat like ignoring that domesticated dogs and cats have long been dear family members and referring to all dogs as wolves or cats as dangerous predators. In fact, when dogs and cats grow up in the wild, totally without human interaction, they pretty much revert to a beastly approach to life just fine. It is we, more than they, who really need a peacefully functioning society for human life to thrive.

The use of right and left in describing political groups goes back to the days of the French Revolution when those representatives primarily supporting the established institutions of royalty and the state church sat to the right of the speaker while those who primarily emphasized the rights of the people sat to the left. History reminds us that this was not a good time and place to be on the right, because "right" heads did most of the rolling. Since then, movements that champion government by one (king or dictator) or the few (oligarchs, aristocracy, wealthy, landed, or clergy) are referred to as the right while those governments claiming to champion the rights of the people at large are referred to as the left.

CHAPTER TWO

WHO ARE THESE PEOPLE?

Conservatives are people who favor maintaining society largely as it currently exists. They're people who prefer the status quo, who see it as desirable that things stay the way they are, and who insist that it is best and wisest to protect society against those who wish to change it. They want to conserve rather than to modify. Be aware, these terms also apply to anything about which there are opinions and not just political issues. If you are building a boat and you choose to use the other boats around you as the pattern to follow, then you are being conservative in boat building design, following the way that seems to you tried and true, taking little risk of mistake. If you, however, want to deviate from that pattern to make some changes you think would improve the performance of the boat, perhaps risking some feature not yet fully developed, then you are embracing a more liberal position on boat building. If you think all the boats currently being made that you could use as a pattern are already too complex and that we should return to dugout canoes, then you have become a reactionary on the subject of boat design. You would have followed a most ancient design for your craft but have created something of little value for what most people use boats for in today's world. If you feel that the boats around you are ridiculously antiquated and that the only boat that you would be interested in is one that has never existed, except in your imagination, then you have become a radical on boat design, with maximum risk of failure.

Knowing that a person is conservative on a certain subject does not guarantee that he will take the conservative position on all subjects. Religious conservatives are those who embrace and support the long-standing orthodoxy of their faith. A devout Catholic could embrace all doctrinal statements he was taught as a child and would be a conservative theologically, and yet personally believe priests should be allowed to get married if they wanted to — a distinctly liberal stance for a Catholic on the question of priestly marriage. So among Catholics, strictly on the internal concerns they have about their church, there are conservatives — traditionalists — and there are liberals — those who want to modify tradition. Also, there are radicals who have great impatience with either doctrinal issues or church polity, and there are reactionaries who feel Vatican II essentially destroyed real Catholicism.

Conservatives mostly think of what is right and smart about the systems that are in place, about the way things are currently being done. The slogan, "America, love it or leave it," — popular decades ago — was an excellent example of this mindset. Conservatives generally see criticism of the established ways as being disloyal and as threatening to upset a correctly functioning system. They feel their interests are best served and argue that everyone in general is better off by protecting the status quo. The conservative position will have had a long history and all the good things that exist in that group will be attributed to the rightness of embracing the conservative ways. Since all the good things we possess have historically come our way by embracing the current ways of thinking and doing, we need to have a strong allegiance to these ways. When conservatives speak, you will hear "conserve," "preserve," "maintain," "support," "defend," "protect" and "leave well enough alone."

Liberals are usually aware of many things they believe are right about the world they live in but tend to give attention to the things they see as wrong or inferior about the systems that are in place. Their statements are most likely to be about things that need to be changed rather than things that need to be left alone. I remember, as a child, the first time I heard an adult say, "If it ain't broke, don't fix it." Since the subject under discussion was automobiles and since I had a great impatience with anything I saw as backward in automotive design, this statement hit me as the dumbest thing I'd ever heard. Of course, there were a lot of things that I liked about the world I lived in. This meant that, though I was conservative about lots of things, I was liberal on the subject of auto design. When liberals speak, you will hear "progress," "change," "modify," "not right," "doesn't work," "unjust," "rights," "improved" and "make things better."

Reactionaries are those who see mainstream conservatives as liberals, as those who have cooperated with liberals to ruin the golden age of the past, when things were as they should be. Reactionaries are composed of those who fault the gradual changes that have occurred in the recent past and the people who supported the changes. They now regret intended or unintended consequences that came about with the changes. They tend to see only the bad that has happened since the changes occurred and believe that, if these changes continue unopposed, greater disaster lies in the future.

Radicals are those who are willing to risk what little value they see in the status quo in order to effect a dramatic transformation in beliefs or the way things are being done. They have a great impatience with the way things are — being consumed by all the wrong in their world.

A group that doesn't fit well in any of these four categories is *anarchists*. These are people who believe that any government is bad and should be eliminated. Over the last couple hundred years, different individuals and small groups have become anarchists. Some have arrived there by being far more extreme reactionaries than even wild-eyed reactionaries would be, while others become anarchists by going off the charts in radicalism. Few of us would see any rational thinking behind championing a total removal of any government where people live together. In a small, well-isolated group, like an extended family or a few friends living close together, very little formal government is needed for a while. Stronger personalities tend to be more influential and to take the lead in making group decisions. However, having millions of people living in close proximity — with each individual being completely free to make any decision he chooses and everyone being expected to work out their differences, with no structure to give constancy to everyday life — staggers the imagination. Therefore, real anarchy as a long-term solution to the challenge of governance has never been embraced for a significant time by any significant group of people. It mostly exists as merely a philosophical construct, an expression of extreme paranoia or a frantic response to someone being agitated to the extreme by what's happening around him. It is a rare society that will tolerate, for very long, anyone who is an actual anarchist, rather than being an anarchist in the privacy of his own disturbed imaginations or in debates and rants. The more dysfunctional government is, the more likely people are to start thinking of anarchy. The more government is perceived as being unfair or too intrusive, the more likely anarchy begins to have an appeal. However, when anarchy is considered in all its practical applications, what most self-proclaimed anarchists really are actually looking for is less government or a government more responsive to their wishes, not a total end to all government.

Throughout recorded history, wherever real anarchy existed, it was a temporary condition and soon replaced with some system of government. Therefore, the question is not "Shall we have government?" but rather "What government shall we have?" Functionally, anarchy can be defined as that period between the death of one government and its replacement by another.

CHAPTER THREE

How Large Are These Groups?

In stable societies or groups which have existed for some time, the largest mass of citizens will be conservatives, those who regularly cooperate with the beliefs they together share and with the systems with which they operate. However accurate or inaccurate, worthy or unworthy, the beliefs or the behavior of any group that has existed over time, it can be expected that most of the people in that group will support their team, mostly liking the way things are and being less concerned about the parts that are troublesome. It would not be unusual for conservatives to make up 60 to 80 percent of society, if there has been a long period of stable history and little influence from outside thinking.

The next largest group is made up of the liberals, those who are more into challenging some of the beliefs of society and changing some of the ways things are done. Most of the ways things are done are accepted by liberals, but there are some, generally minority held, beliefs or behaviors that they want changed. In quiet times where about 70 percent of society are conservatives, about another 20 percent may be liberals. In a more rapidly changing society, conservatives might make up 50 percent and liberals about 30 percent.

During long periods of relative quiet, radicals and reactionaries together would probably make up less than 10 percent. When changes are in the air and liberals are having enough influence to move changes forward more rapidly, there would have been an increase in the number of liberals and more extreme compatriots, the radicals. The most conservative of the conservatives will be much more alarmed at even greater changes that lie ahead and this will create a considerable increase in the number of reactionaries. A rough estimate of the stability of a society is the size of the conservatives or the combined size of conservatives and liberals together. In such a situation, the vast majority will be accepting most of what is seen as right and functional and have a natural caution to not want to endanger all that they depend upon for a good life.

When the foment for change increases, due to people getting increasingly disenchanted in general with the way things are, or when new ideas begin to permeate society, more people begin to move from a conservative to a liberal point of view. Leading this change would usually be some radicals and the percentage of radicals in the group as a whole increases. These changes, of course, will be alarming to the most conservative of the conservatives, and very quickly, the number of those who would correctly be labeled reactionaries will dramatically increase.

Psychologically speaking, stress can be viewed as the

psychological adaptation to change, being forced to reorder parts of your life in order to accommodate new ways of thinking or behaving. People will generally have one of three responses to such changes. Those people who wanted the changes and who are supporting it will be made happier and experience far less stress for the changes. This is acceptance. Those who have little concern about whether things stayed the same or whether they changed are basically going to go with the flow and have only the stress that comes with adapting, practically, to new ways. This is accommodation. Those who distinctly did not want the changes, who fought against them and dislike what is now going on, will be the most stressed of the three. This is rejection. Those who wanted the changes are saying "Hooray," while those who don't have much feelings, one way or another, essentially say "Whatever," or perhaps even "What, me worry?" while the third group has only fighting words to say. You can readily see how changes quickly move from the merely intellectual or philosophical sphere to the emotional and passionate arena. Remember also, the more alarmed people get by what is happening, the more likely they are to become violent. This is well illustrated by the fact that our laws see it as distinctly wrong to physically attack other people, yet understand that very violent behavior is acceptable when you are appropriately alarmed, when someone is physically attacking you or your family — the right of self-defense.

When discontent in a society grows to such extent that the vast majority of people are no longer happy, no longer championing the way things are, primarily focused on the downside and only feel discontent for that society, they have determined that it is time for dramatic changes. They have moved along a continuum from conservative to liberal. During such time, a larger and larger number of people become radical and become much more willing to take huge risks, willing to endanger whatever is of value in the way things are, and willing to roll the dice on life as they know it, hoping that life on the other side of the change will prove to be worth the risks. This would certainly not be a popular time to embrace the reactionary position, with most of society in agreement that things must be significantly changed, moved forward. Nonetheless, reactionary groups can be expected to grow in size and to grow in isolation from the larger society. With all this happening, a great instability permeates society, and if the changes are dramatic enough and rapid enough, a revolution is occurring. This is when society is most unstable.

In summary, society is most stable when the vast majority of people are conservatives or when the conservatives and liberals together make up virtually all of society. In such a situation, there's regular interaction and dialogue between the two groups with virtually any society, over time, gradually undergoing a slow transition into tomorrow. No society remains unchanged forever.

If you are a highway engineer and know that the roadway you are building is going to have to rise ten feet somewhere ahead, if you design the highway where it rises ten feet over the distance of a quarter-mile, a driver going along the new highway would scarcely notice the change. If you design it so that the change occurs over fifty feet, you have an uncomfortable experience for the driver. If you decide to elevate the roadway over a distance of two feet, the driver would essentially be hitting a wall, a ten-foot-high wall. The more gradually changes occur in people's thinking or in the way things are done, the least amount of stress will be felt, the greatest harmony will be enjoyed, the greatest stability will exist and the tiniest amount of society will be in the reactionary or radical groups. The more abrupt the changes, the more upsetting they will be to almost all of society and the more alarmed everyone will become about what is happening. When, for whatever combination of reasons, changes in society are coming very rapidly — usually meaning a larger and larger percentage of liberals are becoming more insistent upon changes and the largest group, the conservatives, are reacting with greater alarm to this increasing threat to what is dear to them, the large central group, that in stable times is made up of conservatives and liberals together, begins to polarize as the middle drains out and flows in two opposite directions. In this case, the conservatives are more and more moving to a reactionary position, and there are few who remain close to the middle to dialogue with the liberals. At the same time, more and more liberals are moving in a radical direction and draining liberals away from the middle to dialogue with conservatives. If this continues long enough you have a society that is essentially composed of reactionaries and radicals, the most dangerous of situations. At such time, most people are forced by the situation to choose which of the two camps they will join. All the power and influence at such a time will be wielded by people who, at stable times, would be seen as too extreme to follow. People who would in stable times be seen as the voice of reason are now seen as the voice of treason. At such a time, a conservative can maintain influence with his people only by, essentially, becoming a reactionary and a liberal can maintain influence with his people only by, essentially, becoming a radical.

Keep in mind that much of the things conservatives champion today were, in the distant past, probably opposed by the conservatives of that day and seen as liberal positions. In the early days of the automobile there was great scorn and alarm by the larger population at the impact these noisy machines were having on society. Laws were passed to ban the use of automobiles or to severely restrict its use by, for instance, requiring a man carrying a flag to walk in front of the automobile to announce its coming. After a couple of decades, however, society had accommodated itself to the reality of the automobile, since virtually all of society now enjoyed it use. Yet there remains, to this day, a reactionary group which feels strongly, for various environmental, monetary, and social reasons, that the automobile is primarily a destructive force in society.

People will also be referred to as *moderates*, usually not as a separate group from the four we've talked about above, but in combination with another term, as in referring to someone as a moderate Republican or a moderate Democrat. Such moderates are usually members of a particular party and embrace, generally, the positions their party embraces with reference to monetary, political, and social issues, but take a fairly pragmatic approach to the changes that are gradually occurring in society and are more interested in practical answers to the issues the nation is facing, rather than more fervently embracing, in a rather absolute way, the ideologies of their party. They are more interested in what works than in being unyielding defenders of intellectual positions.

CHAPTER FOUR

A Quick Look At History

Many of the people who formed and populated the American colonies were disenchanted with the status quo they left behind in Europe. Most of them had some things they specifically wanted to be different in the new world. However, by 1750, most Americans were fairly conservative politically and, likely, religiously and socially as well. They ran their daily lives accepting the rule of England and the installed governments in the various colonies. However, even conservative people, if they feel they are being mistreated for long enough, will begin to think liberal thoughts, will begin to think about how to change the way things are. This will begin a ferment for change, which will pose a challenge for the entrenched power structure. If the power structure hears the disenchantment and responds in a conciliatory way, making gradual changes in response to the protests, then the power structure maintains its hold on society, since most people are naturally conservative. The immediate future is a new conservative order, composed of the way things were, with some minor modifications that lead to the new contentment for the majority of people. If, however, the entrenched powers refuse to pay any attention to the discontent and especially if they respond with what is perceived as ruthlessness, then an even larger percentage of the populace will join the protest, and the demands that were initially somewhat minor will become much more strident. If this continues, the gulf between the power structure and the populace becomes so large that radical voices begin to lead the charge and society enters a very dangerous stage, a stage that could potentially become revolutionary.

When the king of Israel, Solomon, died, his son, Rehoboam, was presented with an ultimatum from a large contingent of his people, which said that if he would relax the more severe policies of his father, they would remain loyal subjects of the new king. If, however, he were to continue the policies of his father, they would break away and form a new nation. Rehoboam consulted his father's advisers who strongly recommended he hear the protests of his people and agree to the desired changes. He also consulted his peers — reared like him in rich luxury — who recommended a response appropriate to their misplaced sense of entitlement. He did not listen to his people, rejected the advice of the elders, and responded to the protesters as his peers suggested. He informed them that his rule would be even heavier than his father's. His kingdom split with the majority of his kingdom, forming a new nation led by his chief adversary.

This is essentially what happened in the American colonies by 1775, with the colonies issuing strong protests to various parts of English rule, and with parliament and the king refusing to move fast enough in making changes for the colonies. At this point, the standoff between the two sides reached a critical point when violence broke out in various locations, creating the Revolutionary War, along with a smaller civil war within it. It could well be argued that had parliament and the king responded in a more cooperative fashion, the majority of the population would not have been so passionately moved to be willing to endanger everything in attempting a violent overthrow of government. Had England been more willing to be flexible, it is quite conceivable that the United States could have remained part of the British Empire, just as Canada and Australia did.

As the revolution rolled across the thirteen colonies, people were not all of the same mind. The vast majority, 20 years earlier, would have been conservative, and the growing group of liberals would have been pushing for changes while staying connected to England. In this setting there would be limited power by radicals and perhaps even less influence by reactionaries. However, by 1775, the majority of people apparently had shifted to the liberal position, an extreme enough liberal position to go into armed combat against the established government! However, even with the majority of Americans supporting the armed struggle, there was a distinct group that still very conservatively opposed the efforts of the majority to go to war and break free from England. As the war years unrolled, those who supported England found themselves in a significant minority and ultimately had to either join the majority, more radical group or find another place to live, such as moving to Canada or back to England.

You will find in Canada, to this day, people who clearly trace their lineage back to the Revolutionary War, when their people refused to cooperate with radical behavior, continued to support the Crown, and still believe that choice was superior to going to war with England.

From a very practical standpoint, government by the people requires freedom of speech, freedom of assembly, freedom of the press, and the right to vote. Given that liberalism grew out of the ferment in Europe, not only over the rule of the aristocracy but also over the rule of the church, freedom of religion was required. This last freedom may be the biggest stumbling block to the spread of democracy in the Middle East today.

As all of us learned our American history growing up, we have largely and proudly embraced the story of how the colonies resisted an unjust rule by England, followed significantly influential leaders and pulled off the American Revolution. This revolution, it seems to me, is one of the few violent revolutions in history that apparently produced a better life for the populace than they had prior to the revolution, and that took a while even then. After all, the Revolutionary War lasted eight years! And even after that, the War of 1812 had to be fought before America was assuredly free from England. Most revolutions destroy societies and give more miserable lives to the people than they had prior to the revolution.

Most Americans, to this day, are glad the revolution occurred and created the United States of America. What came about, by the process described above, has long since become the new conservative. "Give me liberty, or give me death!" is hardly a conservative statement. Such talk in 1775 was perceived as incendiary, treasonable. At that stage, the liberal movement, now moving into its radical stage, was mainly radical talk. Since changes did not occur at this stage, the protest then became physical, in terms of demonstrations by groups of people. Since the response of the power center was still reactionary, then the verbal and physical radical escalated to become the violent radical. The Boston tea party was a radical behavioral response that was standing on the verge of violent response. There seemingly was still time for England to get the message and pull off the policy changes that would have averted war. Even at this stage, most people would have been emotionally more comfortable with a solution that didn't risk massive destruction of their society.

Interestingly, there was already enough history in various European countries to educate all European and American leaders to what could happen when a situation like this was developing. There were plenty of examples of more authoritarian leaders responding in very reactionary fashion, with overwhelming military power, sometimes giving what the rulers thought was success and other times ending in failure. There was, at that time, two schools of thought on how rulers ought to respond by such protest from the subjects.

The most conservative thought was to champion the correctness of the way things were and bring to bear whatever military response was necessary to quell the uprising. This has, throughout human history, been the virtually guaranteed response of a power structure to demands from the people for changes.

The other school of thought could be labeled enlightened self-interest, which held that a ruler, even if completely self-centered, should be wise enough to adapt to the yearnings of his subjects to allow the vast majority of his people — the conservatives — to continue to believe they were better off cooperating with the way things were and not be led astray by more liberal or, certainly, more radical voices. Reading history you find examples of rulers who did the first and examples of rulers who do the second, and can see the success or failure in each case.

In the middle of World War I, massive social foment in Russia led to civil war between the whites and reds, in which the royalty was overthrown, a communist government was established and the royal family assassinated. During the civil unrest in Italy in the '20s following World War I, Mussolini established a right-wing dictatorship known as fascism.

Prior to World War I, Germany was one of the most educated and technologically advanced countries in existence, with the government headed by a king (Kaiser). Coming out on the losing end of the war created a Germany, which, while still possessing all these advantages, had great emotional turmoil that tore at the fabric of society. The economy deteriorated year-by-year until, by 1930, most Germans had lost faith in their government as it was currently functioning. This left the people searching for a better way. The better ways being suggested were that society needed to move to the left or to the right. Various groups on the right competed with each other as well as competing with the left. The same struggle was going on among the groups on the left. As is typical in such a situation, as emotions overwhelmed rational thought, the words became more violent and full-blown physical violence broke out. When one extreme group becomes violent, it seems necessary that the opposite extreme seeks to top the violence.

Various reactionary groups arose and various radical groups arose, draining off the big middle and leading to greater polarization. By the early '30s, Germany essentially found itself with a choice between two violent groups, the Nazis on the right and the Communists on the left. The Nazis, under the leadership of Hitler, won the day. His government then crushed the communists and anyone else on the right, on the left, or in the center who might get in his way. In this, he was also following the example of Mussolini's fascism in Italy.

During the Spanish Civil War of the 1930s, the government was overthrown and a right wing dictatorship was established by Francisco Franco. From the latter '20, through World War II, there was an enduring civil war in China between the forces of Chiang Kai-shek and the communist forces of Mao Zedong, with mainland China, in the end, becoming communist. In the late '50s in Cuba, a civil war against the military dictatorship broke out that led to a leftist victory and the establishment of a communist government. The primary international concern of the United States from the end of World War II until the fall of the Soviet Union was the fervent drive to stop the spread of communism in the other countries of the world. This usually left us supporting right wing dictators as partners in anti-Communist wars.

The history of the twentieth century is rife with peoples becoming disenchanted with the policies of their government, polarizing into right and left and undergoing warfare to create a new government by a victorious right or a victorious left. Whatever the yearnings were that led the people to such rebellious behavior, their individual freedoms were usually not improved by all they went through, protesting their existing governments. Usually what came out at the end was a totalitarian right or a totalitarian left government, in which the rights of the people were essentially, reduced to them having only the right to be silent and cooperate with the new government.

CHAPTER FIVE

A Little More History: The Big Two

Most significant changes that occur in the history of societies happen by the coming together of two forces, the first practical and the second philosophical. Practical changes, which at times also include technological changes, occur as people are developing better ways of operating their daily lives or are increasingly becoming disenchanted as a group with the way they are being treated. Philosophical changes occur as leading thinkers and opinion shapers begin to think about the values and structures of their society and begin to champion new ways of conceiving of and structuring society. The American Revolution occurred primarily because of the practical everyday changes the majority of the colonists wanted in the laws by which their governments operated. This would have been reason enough for changes to be attempted. However, of perhaps equal importance was the intellectual foment that was sweeping the West, fed by those who were strongly questioning the validity of the royalty and championing the rights of more common people to determine their fate.

The existing governments throughout all of human history had primarily been "government of the rich, by the rich, and for the rich." This means that all political power as well as everything of economic value was in the hands of the wealthy few. The military and police arms of the government were more tasked with keeping everyone in subjection than with equitable enforcement of laws. The new ferment was beginning to move Western society in the direction of creating societies embracing the concept "government of the people, by the people, and for the people," even if it were not spelled out. These two conditions, occurring simultaneously, appealed strongly enough to the disparate groups of society for a sufficient energy to be created to propel the colonies through years of warfare to create such a country.

Had there been the practical desires of the people, without strong philosophical undergirding, there likely would not have been enough energy fomented to carry the war through to victory. Even if there had been enough unrest to throw out the existing rulers, the government that they would have created would likely still have been a government of aristocracy, with laws made and enforced by the few at the top of society. However, had there been only the philosophical campaign of freedom for the masses, without large-scale social discontent, there likely would not have been enough passion created to overthrow the government, given the natural conservative nature of the majority of the citizenry.

Most massive upheavals in various societies throughout human history have been brought about by the outside invasion of armies from other nations rather than the people choosing to overthrow their own government. The people's choice, in such situations, was to embrace their own royalty and hope to be protected by their government and its armies. When warfare broke out, you went to war to try to survive and repel the invasion. If you successfully did repel the invasion then you continued, loyally, to support your rulers. If you failed to repel the invasion, you then had a new ruler that you then had to obey and embrace for the next segment of your life. In either outcome, you lived in a society controlled by rulers.

An excellent example is the Roman Empire of two thousand years ago. As Oregon State's Marcus Borg points out, the Roman Empire was a domination system, conquering and maintaining obedience to its empire by the amount of horror it was demonstrably ready to immediately visit upon any and all who resisted its invasions or opposed any of the governments it instituted in the conquered territories.

Also, within a given society, there could be power struggles between different factions of the ruling elite, such that society erupted into warfare with ordinary people choosing sides and following different leaders, living through a civil war until there was a winning side. Then a new royalty was established, which the commoners would then support for the next stage of their country's existence. Whether society was dramatically changed by the invasion of an outside group or by warfare among its own leaders, there was no philosophical difference to mix in, to change the fundamental way governments functioned. In both cases, government was still ruled by aristocracy. It is seen as most fortunate that, when the thirteen colonies became exceedingly frustrated with the way the rulers were ruling, there was at the same time a tidal wave of revolutionary thought rolling across Europe and the colonies, infecting the thinking and political life of each of those nations, in varying degrees.

The revolutionary thought, that came to threaten all the existing governments in Europe at that time, was the claim that each individual citizen has rights equal to any other citizen and that government can exist only with the approval of its citizens, rather than through inheritance, warfare, or supposed divine determination. Thus, the individual citizen was free to choose for himself on a variety of issues that had, before that, been decided for him by imposed government.

This philosophy, emphasizing the freedom of the individual, was referred to as liberal thinking — from the Latin word *liberalis*, meaning free. This is also where we get the term *liberty*. The coming together of the very practical and the very philosophical — pushing for change — created the energy necessary to throw off the old government and to even change the old ways of thinking about government. It generated the momentum to push through to the creation of a new government, but more importantly for the colonists and the rest of humanity (my opinion here), a new type of government that would attempt to successfully address the practical grievances of the governed, and to install in that government the revolutionary philosophies so necessary to the successful completion of the war.

However, the coming together of these two forces, social unrest and a revolutionary philosophy, does not necessarily create an improved life for the people or establish a government more responsive to their needs. The Russian Revolution of 1917 came about through great societal unrest, created by the way the czarist government had been ruling for generations. This foment could well have brought about a civil war with the current royal family being overthrown and a new ruling elite taking charge. The people would likely have done what most nations have always done and chosen sides in the power struggles of princes. However, a powerful revolutionary philosophy was thrown into the mix that ended not only with the royalty being overthrown but with a new type of government being installed, in this case a communist government.

However revolutionary, however radical communist ideology may have appeared to most Russians in the midst of the revolution, fifty years later it was the conservative position of the vast majority of Russian citizens, who embraced communist ideology and expressed loyalty to their leaders. This was a government that typified itself as being the savior for the people in granting them freedom. History would clearly demonstrate that, once again, what was created was another totalitarian government with a different privileged elite — the communist party leaders — ruling.

Freedom was an important word in communist revolutionary propaganda, just as freedom has always been an important word in the history of the United States and other Western democracies. However, whereas freedom in the United States promised its citizens the freedom to speak, to think, to worship, and to self-determine, freedom in communist countries was primarily promised not as *freedom to* but as *freedom from* — as in freedom from hunger and freedom from warfare. It's interesting that different communist governments have included the terms "Peoples' Republic of" or "the Democratic Peoples' Republic of," even though none of them have had government by the people or have been operated according to democratic principles. After fifty years of existence, however, virtually all these governments were supported by the vast majority of their citizens, conservatives who were loyal to their leadership and to the philosophy used to justify the power of the rulers.

When liberal currents swept across the Soviet Union in the late '70s and '80s so that the communist government was toppled and replaced by an elected government and various nations broke away from the Soviet Union, leaving Russia its own nation, the conservative communist government was replaced with an optimistic attempt at democracy. During the time of social and economic upheaval that followed, more and more Russians began to long for the security and constancy, and the international prestige, of the old communist regime, and to regret having been led astray by the liberal element preaching freedom and democracy. In this period of turmoil, where a mature democratic government had not firmly taken root, a leader — who represented the longing to return to the old ways, to the tried and true Soviet past — former KGB agent Vladimir Putin, came to power, becoming about as close as one can come to being a dictator in what would appear, on paper, to be a democracy

CHAPTER SIX

A PSYCHOLOGICAL DETOUR

There has long been curiosity about what makes people conservative or liberal and especially what makes them radical or reactionary. Most people championing each of these four positions do not generally explain it based on their genetics or natural tendencies on how they view life. Yet philosophers and psychologists have long sought to understand what makes people primarily embrace one of these ways of viewing life. It's also hoped, by the most pragmatic among them, that they could then predict people's behavior and, better yet, be able to better control it. Many of these very practical philosopher-psychologists are popularly known now as political consultants.

It seems very clear that most humans, most of the time, want stability and are willing to surrender some freedom in order to not have warfare. The history of most peoples will include relatively long periods of stability, even if individual freedom scarcely exists, interspersed with occasional periods of warfare, either invasion or revolution. When there is chaos in the land, most citizens will settle for losing some of their freedom, some of their rights, to someone who can bring some order and some security to the land. Historically, it seems that, only after stability and order have been restored, the question of freedom and justice begins to be addressed and acted on. Where chaos exists, pushing for freedoms and rights seems a reckless luxury. When a revolution occurs, the new order has a brief time to establish a functioning government which approximates the longings of its people that led to the revolution. Where this fails to happen in a brief enough period of time, either renewed chaos or a new totalitarianism takes over. In America, a middle course between chaos and totalitarianism was steered by the creation of a strong central government responsive to democratic ideals.

Young people coming into adulthood tend to be in the most liberal period of their lives. They are more likely to struggle against the restrictions that have been placed on them and want the freedom to do what they want to do. They're more likely to be critical of the thinking that justifies the restrictions. Also, they are, probably, in the least cautious time of their lives and taking risks tends to be exciting and invigorating.

In the book, *The Struggle of the Soul*, Union Theological Seminary's Lewis J. Sherrill divides adulthood into three sections, young adulthood, middle years, and old age. A summary word can be used to describe each stage.

Identification typifies young adulthood. This is the time of expansion when we want to see what the world has to offer, we want to try new experiences, meet new friends, see what's over the horizon, read new philosophies, and in general run with exuberance through the world before us. This openness to new thinking and new behavior hits precisely at the time when millions of young people are being influenced by the thinking they encounter in whatever media they choose, in living life on their own for the first time and in higher education. During this time, the influence of peers largely replaces the influence of parents. This likely is not the most conservative time of life for most people.

Maturation best typifies the middle years. When one has searched and experienced enough of what the world has to offer and has made the necessary choices on how to build his kingdom, he then builds, consolidates, and manages his world, forming alliances with other similar people, such as a spouse and friends, who are primarily interested in a stable but growing future. Such years are much more driven by the desire to build, conserve and protect all that is valuable. This creates a much more conservative approach to life.

However, for many, the desire to build includes the desire for creating what they see as a more desirable society, therefore having them support liberal causes.

Old age is best typified by *Simplification*. During this stage, whatever kingdom has been created and maintained over the previous decades becomes too much to manage any longer. There is little desire left to explore the new, merely the desire to protect the basic essentials of one's life. As life moves through the later middle years into old age, more and more possessions, desires, and systems of thought are deemed unessential and dropped from consideration. As Baylor Prof. P. D. Brown said,

"When we get old, we don't so much change, as we just get more like ourselves." The older we get, the more we become just the essential core of who we really are. This tends then to be the most conservative time of life.

Voting patterns tend to indicate this fairly predictable trend in the way a population votes over its lifetime. This doesn't mean that young people are necessarily liberals, for among them will be all four of the political categories we're talking about. But there will be, for a large group, this fairly predictable trend on various issues, political, economic, religious, social, and relational. It has long been noted that a large percentage of teenagers and young adults will be embracing the most liberal sexual values they will have yet will, when they are parents of children and teenagers, find themselves in perhaps the most conservative period of their lives, in terms of sexual values, especially if they have daughters.

It is noteworthy how many protest movements for the last hundred years have been led primarily by students and other young people. Rarely do you find massive protests primarily driven by middle-aged people, who are much more cautious, much more aware of what they could lose, and much more involved in just making life work, with all its responsibilities. The youth, with much less load on their shoulders, feel a freedom and even an exhilaration in striking out in new directions. This incaution usually alarms their parents.

When the movement to drop the voting age in the United States from twenty-one to eighteen was being debated, the great fear of conservatives was that giving the vote to these scarcely-out-of-childhood, immature impulsives would significantly affect the outcome of any number of elections, in a liberal direction. This fear certainly seemed well founded, given the years of media coverage of young people involved in civil rights, antiwar, antigovernment, anticorporate, feminist, and environmental protests. However, from most indications, it seems these fears were greatly overblown. Seemingly, enough young people either didn't vote, were somewhat conservative on the voting issues or were largely influenced by their parents beliefs or allegiances so that there was no revolution at the voting booth.

It seems that young people currently are more likely to be conservative on political and economic issues than they are on social, sexual, and relationship issues.

Research seems to suggest that while the majority of people basically live their adulthood as conservatives, a definite percentage tend to live their entire lives with a more questioning attitude toward their world, leading them to embrace more liberal ways of viewing the world. This tends to be rooted in childhood, frequently quite early. Most parents of more than one child, if asked, could identify the more traditional child contrasted with the child more questioning of parental desires and thought. This is a good predictor of how these children will likely approach life in their adult years.

A possible genetic factor influencing a person to be conservative or liberal is that conservatives tend to, seemingly naturally, be more risk averse than do liberals.

Having, for decades, dealt with people's ways of thinking, it seems to me that rational, mentally stable and responsible people by the millions could be found all across the spectrum from extremely conservative to extremely liberal. I say this because, sometimes, the heat of debate suggests that people of a given position must be unbalanced or irrational, or have evil intentions. I have experienced so many people with good intentions and healthy values strongly embracing and supporting the whole range of positions on various political, religious, economic and social issues. Admittedly, I have also seen people of various base motives showing up in each of these groups.

It is also possible for the unbalanced or irrational to appear in any of these groups. It seems to me that mental disease seems to have the most likely impact in support of either a reactionary or a radical cause. It is outside the scope of this book to deal at length with various maladies, but one example is the issue of paranoia. The more paranoid a person, the more likely rational discussion or clear facts in evidence are to be unable to alter beliefs or desires. Also the more paranoid the person, the more likely any opposition will be seen as the enemy, as treason. The longer this runs, the more isolated such a person feels, convinced a larger and larger percentage of people are against him. Of course, the more his rantings gain public attention, the more people are alarmed by him and likely to respond in ways that prove, to him, that he was right all along, that everyone was against him. In this situation, his paranoia has become a self-fulfilling prophecy. The increasing fear that is generated significantly increases the likelihood of him one day engaging in violent behavior.

Group paranoia may be the greatest danger posed by serious political polarization. Statements of the most unbalanced or manipulative on the left and on the right extremes become self-fulfilling prophecies drawing larger and larger numbers to embrace their alarming misrepresentations. As each group responds to the outlandish allegations with equally outlandish allegations of their own, mutually created paranoia actually creates a mutually self-fulfilling prophecy greatly endangering the stability of the society. At such a time cooler heads are desperately needed. Yet anything said by the cooler heads — people not embracing the extreme right or the extreme left — is rejected as a sellout to the opposite wing.

Alfred Adler pointed out that people will have courage to continue to press forward in creating a good life, solving problems, and establishing relationships as long as they believe in themselves and believe they could work with other people to create and maintain a life worth living in a good world. He pointed out that when people do not have the courage or have lost it, when they have become "dis-couraged," there is no trust that they could be sufficiently effective with other people to succeed in life according to the way people think life should be. A person who turns to crime likely believes either that he does not have the capability or the society does not give the opportunity for him to have a profitable life, staying in the bounds of the law. To the degree that someone believes he is too lacking or the system is too stacked against him, the courage to prevail to success will not exist, and deviant avenues may be pursued.

So too, when a nation's people either feel helpless to be effective in enough of what is important in life or feel the society in which they live is so stacked against them that they lack the courage to continue to work with all other elements of their society to resolve contentious issues, then in their discouragement, they are likely to begin to move to a more extreme, more isolating position. The greater their rejection of the larger society and the greater the helplessness they are increasingly feeling, the greater the likelihood they are willing to consider violent means to correct the situation. For the vast majority of people who occupy the conservative and liberal middle range of society, violence is alarming and is strongly rejected as an acceptable behavior, as an appropriate problem-solver.

Interestingly, even though reactionaries and radicals are the most polar opposites in their beliefs on specific issues, they tend to be on the same page when it comes to the readiness and the necessity for violence. Also interesting, while most terrorist concerns of Americans center around Islamists threats, Homeland Security lists homegrown terrorists as the biggest immediate threat to security in the United States. It seems a given that violent members of both the extreme right and the extreme left hope to alarm as many citizens as possible and pull them from the center to join them in a readiness for violence, to accomplish, even with much destruction, an extreme goal. It is also to be expected that however much the leaders of such groups speak of freedom, liberty, and rights, they are themselves believers in a totalitarian structure for their own organization, with them the ruling elite.

Since people so easily get set in their ways and usually develop strong loyalties to their tribe, cuisine, philosophy, beliefs, and even habits, it is perhaps amazing when any majority chooses to go through the extreme discomfort of embracing a new philosophy and revamping their very lives to install radical thinking. Only rarely has a system of thought been powerful enough to, on its own, remake a society in its image. Virtually always the new philosophy only has a chance if the society is already in turmoil and great dissatisfaction exists throughout the land. Even rarer is for a philosophy to significantly alter society without using violent means to accomplish its change, but it has happened.

Compared to all the governmental changes that have occurred around the globe during the last two hundred plus years, it is amazing that, with the United States going through all the changes in industrialization, economy, immigration, geographic expansion, world wars, and smaller wars, it has had only one Civil War to tear the country apart. When the phrase "All men are created equal and endowed by their Creator with certain unalienable rights," was coined, *men* was defined, practically, as being adult, free, white, landed, male, member of the official church, and in some cases, married. The history of the United States has been a steady expansion of the term *men* to apply to all adult citizens of the country, a wildly radical idea in 1776.

There are many factors that have worked together to accomplish such a feat. It is well beyond the scope of this book to try to explain how that happened. It is my personal belief that one of the key ingredients in this accomplishment has been our constant return to the thinking that was embodied in our original documents and the thinking of those who wrote those documents and formed the governments the documents described. These papers contained concepts far beyond the realities of government in the new nation as it originally was organized and functioned. They have, throughout the history of the United States, continually called us to create a better nation than what actually exists at any prior time. As is true of so many great writings, these documents continually hold up an ideal against which we can compare our performance. They continually challenge us to "create a more perfect union."

From the very formation of the United States, there have been real opportunities for the whole experiment to get derailed into chaos or dictatorship. Many have been the times when wise observers truly feared that this whole fragile attempt to form and preserve a nation of, by, and for the people was in serious danger of coming to destruction.

Points of extreme polarization have occurred many times in the history of the United States with each crisis resolving itself into a period of relative calm and stability. Each crisis was accompanied by great group paranoia in each of the extremes with the most dire accusations and feared consequences spoken by each group toward the other. As each such crisis was resolved, the vast majority of citizens enjoyed the calm that existed until the next major crisis. Fortunately, the United States has experienced throughout its history a gradual progress toward a better government for its citizens. The process seems rather like waves on the water with crisis peaks occurring around various issues, which are then resolved in an improved society. Even the polarization that led up to the Civil War did not permanently end the United States of America.

That this government has endured through all these crises is explained by a cluster of realities philosophical and practical. Perhaps there is no better example of the value of "creative tension" than the fact that the United States exists as it does today, even after all this tumultuous history.

CHAPTER SEVEN

ORGANIZATIONS

The following are the revolutions that led to left-wing, or radical, governments:

- Russia
1922-1991
Vladimir Lenin
Union of Soviet Socialist Republics

- China
1930s–Current
Mao Zedong
People's Republic of China

- Vietnam
1930s–Current
Ho Chi Minh
Socialist Republic of Vietnam

- North Korea
1945–Current
Kim Il-Sung
Democratic People's Republic of Korea

- Cuba
1959–Current
Fidel Castro
Republic of Cuba

The following are the revolutions that led to right wing, or reactionary, governments:

- Italy
1922–1943
Benito Mussolini
Italy

- Japan
1932–1945
Empire of Great Japan

- Germany
1933–1945
Adolph Hitler
Greater German Reich

- Spain
1936–1975
Francisco Franco

Spain

- Cuba

1950–1959

Fulgencia Batista

Republic of Cuba

The following are th left wing, or radical, groups in the US:

- Student Nonviolent Coordinating Committee (SNCC)
- Black Panther Party (BPP)
- Symbionese Liberation Army (SLA)
- Students for a Democratic Society (SDS)

The following are the right wing, or reactionary, groups in the US:

- Ku Klux Klan (KKK)
- America Nazi party (ANP)
- John Birch Society (JBS)

The following groups are currently active:
Where would you classify them?

- Operation Rescue
- Sea Shepherd Conservation Society (SSCS)
- The Libertarian Party
- People for the Ethical Treatment of Animals (PETA)
- National Rifle Association (NRA)
- Justice Party USA

- National Organization of Women (NOW)
- Sovereign Nation
- Boston Tea Party (BTP)
- National Organization for the Repeal of Marijuana Laws (NORML)
- Constitution Party
- Freedom Alliance

CHAPTER EIGHT

How Ready Are We To Become Extreme?

The last century in American politics has mostly followed the pattern given in Chapter 3, with long periods of stability, where conservatives and liberals struggle together to govern. In this setting, radicals and reactionaries were mostly consigned to the sidelines of American politics. When certain issues were emotional enough and divisive enough to begin stressing the large middle, the more extreme positions began to be supported by larger numbers of citizens.

An excellent example was the national response to the Great Depression. In the early '30s, as the depression ground on, more and more citizens began to lose faith in the ability of either party to be able to handle the national economic chaos successfully. People who otherwise were quite conservative and had long had faith in government to wisely govern began to open their ears to people peddling more extreme plans. Farmers have traditionally been among the most conservative of citizens and yet farmers across America began to discuss what merit there might be in embracing some form of Marxism as a rational solution. During this time, millions embraced the promise of the Townsend plan to bring relief to the elderly poor and bring the country out of depression, however much the plan was panned by virtually all economists.

Millions of Americans followed the media accounts of numbers of bank robbers, officially deploring the criminal behaviors. But with so many losing their homes and farms to bank foreclosures and the thieves hitting those same banks, these very citizens also found themselves elevating the daring thieves to hero status.

As World War II ramped up, the overwhelming conservative position on international involvement among American citizens was isolation, the insistence that we would stay out of European and Asian wars and leave it to the rest of the world to fight each other if they wanted to. Franklin Roosevelt campaigned without revealing how strongly he felt that it was necessary for us to enter the war to stop the spread of right-wing militarism across the globe. The Japanese attack on Pearl Harbor and the Japanese declaration of war decided for us that we were, indeed, in the Asian war. The following declaration of war by Japan's axis partner, Germany, decided for us that we were, indeed, in the European war as well. Had the Japanese not attacked Pearl Harbor, how much longer would it have taken for the majority of Americans to move from isolationism and vote to go to war against Japan? Even after Pearl Harbor, had Germany not followed with its own declaration of war against the United States, how much time would have passed before we, on our own, would have been ready to declare war against Nazi Germany that was not attacking us, merely tearing up Europe?

Interestingly, following World War II we did not return to the strong isolationism of the '30s, electing instead to proactively pursue a path of military preparedness that has led us to be the world's superpower. Throughout America's history, a strong majority has consistently initially been strongly conservative when presented with any new social, political, economic, or military trend, even though many of these trends have now become standard.

As various issues become much more prominent in the electorate's attention, a real oddity in American political life occurs — the creation of a strong third party offering a serious alternative to the usual two parties. Each of these issues has some impact on the big middle, but when people become frustrated with the pace of influencing the middle, and a popular enough leader surfaces, then a strong third political party is created, forcing the middle to take the third-party more seriously.

The growing success of the civil rights movement, a powerful liberal crusade, in the '50s and '60s brought about, perhaps, the greatest polarization, up till that time, in the twentieth century. Racial segregationist governors such as Orval Faubus in Arkansas; John Bell Williams in Mississippi, Lester Maddox in Georgia, and George Wallace in Alabama very successfully ran for election and reelection throughout the '50s and '60s, resisting pressure from the federal courts and federal administrations, both Democratic and Republican, to dismantle Jim Crow. The strength of this reactionary movement was well illustrated by the 1968 presidential election in which George Wallace showed how powerful a third-party candidate could be, if an issue was polarizing enough to a large segment of the population. The populist strategies Wallace used during his runs for president became the pattern for those who would be successful, in the following decades, in winning presidencies and governorships, especially with voters in the south.

If the race between Republicans and Democrats is close enough, even a very small third party can shift the outcome of an election. After the 2000 presidential election, the nation waited while a cliffhanger drama unfolded in Florida, where fewer than one thousand votes separated George Bush and Al Gore. What is most remembered about the outcome of that election was that the Supreme Court of the United States decided the winner. What is less remembered was the candidacy of third-party candidate Ralph Nader, running on the Green Party ticket. Gore supporters appealed to Nader to drop his candidacy so as not to drain off potential votes from the Democratic ticket, the party most environmentalists supported. Nader refused to drop out of the race and garnered 97,000 votes in Florida. It was assumed that the majority of those 97,000 would have been cast for the Democratic candidate, given Florida's electoral votes to Al Gore and made him the new president of the United States. Though the environmentalist party had little national power, it was, perhaps, in the right place at the right time to determine who would be the new president of the United States.

A real oddity in American third parties occurred in the 1992 presidential election where Ross Perot won a larger percentage of popular votes than any third party since Teddy Roosevelt. His candidacy was so strong that both Democrats and Republicans were fearful he might throw the election to the other party by drawing away their faithful to his new party. The oddity was that his multi-issue party drew more than half its support from moderates with the other half split about equally between liberals and conservatives. In the end, he drew about the same number of people from each of the two major parties, therefore not tipping the final result to either party.

In multiparty parliamentary democracies, it's typical for a tiny party to cast the deciding vote on an issue. Our long tradition of having only two powerful parties competing and compromising with each other rarely gives a minority party veto power.

Other highly divisive issues that followed the civil rights movement were the antiwar movement, the feminist movement and the environmental movement. The most divisive issue, since 1972, was the legalization of abortion. This has been the most polarizing issue since then, until concern over the economy dramatically bypassed it in the fall of 2008. The debate over the economy has become the number one issue since.

CHAPTER NINE

THE WAY WE WERE

Decades ago, a Korean colleague of mine would regularly share with me his observations about the differences between American and Korean cultures. He said if you walk around the typical American classroom and ask the children "What do you want to be?" you will get answers like "I want to be a fireman," "teacher," "doctor," or such. If you walk around a Korean classroom and ask the same question, the answer you will get is "I want to be a good boy." Each boy you ask will give the same answer, "I want to be a good boy." My colleague was using this to illustrate what a striking difference the American mentality of individualism and self-determination was compared to the Korean mentality of obedience and responsibility to your family and history.

It is difficult for Americans to perceive how virtually universal was the indoctrination of citizens, globally, to be subservient to their leaders. It wasn't so much that individualism was frowned upon as it was that the idea of individual rights of self-determination was scarcely approached by the vast majority of citizens in organized societies. Seemingly, this was pervasively true in Asian societies and largely true even in the West.

To the degree that specific philosophies were needed to justify the reality that the only people with rights were the royalty, it was pointed out that this was always the way humanity was that those who occupied ruling positions were clearly the superior people who should be in charge, that royalty owned their titles and possessions by inheritance, or that the divine right of kings meant that opposing the king was opposing God. Add to that the pervasive reality that resisting your rulers was somewhere between pointlessly stupid and outright suicidal and that parents from birth strongly instilled in their children the necessity of being absolutely obedient to parents and to those whom the parents obeyed, one can see that the conservative approach to life was virtually the universal approach. Certainly, the rulers wished it this way and all others daily lived with the obvious reality of their real station in life.

The story is told of a zookeeper walking through the zoo with a group of visitors and talking to them about the various animals. They were standing in front of the lion's cage when one of the visitors, with some real alarm, said that the bars holding in the lion looked so spindly that she thought the lion could break through them and escape. The zookeeper responded nonchalantly, "Yes, he could. But the lion doesn't know that."

Zig Zeigler talked about training fleas. He said if you put them in a box with a lid, they would jump and hit the lid and eventually stop jumping. Then you could remove the lid and the fleas would stay in the box.

Throughout recorded history, most of the ferment against the existing rulers was channeled in support of competing royals, not in support of the rights of peons. When people dreamed of freedom they dreamed of throwing off the yoke of a foreign government which had conquered them, reduced many to actual slavery, and held the rest of them in virtual slavery to the whims of the victorious. Conquerors learned to pacify conquered tribes by either installing new, obedient local aristocrats who were willing to keep their people in line, or more brutally, by executing the aristocracy and intelligentsia or carrying them away into captivity and dispersing them throughout the larger empire, thereby eliminating the tribal mentality that might provide a rallying point for future resistance to the new empire (as in the Old Testament story).

This doesn't mean that all people happily embraced such a reality. Individually, each of us wants to not be mistreated, as is well illustrated by every established society having laws against murder and robbery, at the citizen-to-citizen level. Historically, however, to the degree there was rule of law, aristocracy simply wrote the laws to allow them to have whatever they wanted and to keep the populace, at large, disfranchised. Essential to this rule of law was the reality that disobedience to the will of the aristocracy was criminal behavior, punishable by the police and military. In such a system, the local ruler could claim at least partial ownership of everything in his domain, provided he had the power to back it up. (An attorney friend of mine shared with me that, decades ago in his first day of class in criminal law at Harvard Law, crime was defined as, "that which the upper class does not do.")

In such a world, there were occasional malcontents who would arise and begin to trouble the waters. History includes the stories of many such troublers, though most troublers were surely snuffed out long before they could become well enough known to be recorded. Whatever trouble could be caused for the rulers was largely localized and posed little threat to rulers in other areas. There was virtually no likelihood of widespread class warfare. There also was little or no philosophical underpinning to support such a movement.

Major changes in society usually come about when there is a combining of new thinking with new technology, which together create a momentum that cannot be stopped. The new thinking that ordinary people ought to be free, or liberated, from enslavement to ruling aristocracy began to be propounded in various areas of Europe from the fourteenth century onward by religious, political, and economic writers. As long as each troubler could be silenced by imprisonment or death, such thinking posed little threat to the ruling elite. Once, however, these thinkers had access to printing presses the game changed forever. Now revolutionary ideas could be spread to any others who could read or hear the words read to them. Even if you imprisoned or executed the writer, once the word was printed and scattered abroad, the ideas had a life of their own. Thus the concept that "The pen is mightier than the sword" began to be proven true, wholesale.

Among those who populated the colonies of the new world were a definite percentage who had already voted, with their feet, against the constraints of life as they knew it in Europe. They were, perhaps, already thinking more about rights and freedom than the average European. Most of the colonial leaders were educated in the classics and the intellectual ferment of the Enlightenment. Writers, such as John Locke, claiming that rulers should only rule by permission of the people, were influential in the thinking of those who came to the fore in leading the challenges against mother England. Liberty was shorthand for the rights of free individuals.

When the discontent became strong enough for a large enough percentage of the colonists, they moved from their expected conservative position (remain loyal and obedient to the powers that be) and became more open to liberal ideas of freedom and self-determination. Without enormous discontent these ideas would have remained primarily concepts.

But years of warfare, culminating in the formation of a new nation, meant that those ideas, which in the not-too-distant past would have been seen as radical, were now embraced in the very founding documents of the nation. Fifty years prior, the colonists were loyal subjects of the Crown. After the upheaval, the new government was forbidden to grant any titles of royalty. The radical quickly became the new majority. This, of course, didn't prevent any number of individuals or groups, then and now, from dreaming of establishing themselves as royalty, with or without the official titles, rather than fully embracing the democratic ideals of the founding documents. The European countries from which the colonists came all had state churches. State churches were forbidden in the founding documents of the new nation.

Governments formed on democratic principles can take a variety of forms. A small enough group of people could operate with a pure democracy where they all, together, discuss and decide what to do about each issue. This would obviously prove extremely unwieldy in nations with millions of citizens, and therefore, some form of representative democracy has to be established. The United States is obviously a republic rather than a pure democracy. This seems to have worked pretty well for quite a long time, and seems to have had wide influence for democracy around the globe as an example to other peoples.

This, in spite of the fact that during the Revolutionary War period and following, sharp opponents of the breakaway colonies, primarily in England and on the continent, ridiculed the hypocrisy of Americans claiming that all men are created equal and endowed by their Creator with certain unalienable rights, including the right to life, liberty, and the pursuit of happiness, while still denying freedom to the masses of slaves within the colonies.

By now, Americans as a whole have so embraced the basic concepts of our founding fathers that it is easy for them to forget that a huge percentage of the world's populace may not share such desires. Those who are raised in totalitarian governments that successfully shield their citizens from outside communication are steeped in blind loyalty to the authorities. An obvious example of this currently is North Korea. The Iron

Curtain was the most obvious example of this for decades in the twentieth century, but controlling the information flow in order to control the populace is standard practice wherever freedom, on a large scale, is denied. This is easily seen by looking at totalitarian regimes around the globe today. The Internet, being much more difficult to police than other forms of media, has proven an enormous worry to dictators, globally.

Another group that continues to be a head scratcher for many Americans is the millions of citizens in Muslim nations who believe Western ideals, such as the ones that were used in forming the United States, are anathema. Many Western leaders have long been hesitant to push for democratic reforms in Middle Eastern governments run by strong dictators. The fear is that once these populations are allowed to vote into power the government they want, they will simply vote in single party governments run by fundamentalist clergy.

The Iranian revolution certainly was no example of government change by democratic voting process. Yet the majority of people supported the creation of what is, essentially, a totalitarian regime. The great fear about all this is that several nations gaining the vote while under overwhelming influence by strongly reactionary mullahs will then quickly use that vote to elect and establish governments similar to that in Iran.

My Korean colleague was describing the Korea of the '40s and '50s. South Korea since then has been undergoing a steady movement toward Western ways of thinking. However, it seems quite clear that the citizens of North Korea are stuck about where they were a century ago. It seems safe to expect that the vast majority of those citizens interpret their world pretty much as their rulers want them to. To whatever degree there are citizens who embrace more radical ideals, they are probably far too realistic to do much more than keep their thoughts to themselves

Attempting to establish democracy in nations that have no history of freedoms has proven to be risky business. However much we Americans may value their freedoms, we need to keep in mind that untold millions around the world simply do not want Western democracy. At the present time, they want strongmen to rule them. However radically things may have changed in much of the world, in some places and in some ways, things seem not to have changed it all.

CHAPTER TEN

When Conservatives Become Radical and When Radicals Become Conservative

The term *radical* is used two different ways in discussing politics and government. The fourfold classification here uses radical to refer to those to the left of liberals, those who want even more extreme changes or much more rapid movement in changing government.

A much broader use of the term *radical* in everyday conversation as well as in political discussion is to call radical virtually anything that is dramatically different from the norm or to actions that require much more destruction in order to achieve an ultimately desired outcome. When dealing with physical health issues, for instance, the conservative approach to health problems is to make some minor adjustments in lifestyle. A less conservative approach would be to make significant changes in diet and exercise. An even more liberal approach would be to employ physical therapy or take prescription medication. When it's determined that these measures will fail, then the radical alternative, surgery, is used. Surgery is seen as a radical solution to treating a physical malady. A physician who tends to use surgery as a solution as frequently as possible is seen as knife happy.

Likewise, continuing to run your marriage as you have always run it is a conservative approach (which is a luxury you may be able to afford if both partners seem okay with the way things are). Reading books and articles, listening to Oprah or Dr. Phil or going to a marriage counselor are liberal attempts to improve or save a marriage. Divorce is an extreme, a radical, solution to marital unhappiness. Divorce is the marital equivalent of major surgery for the body — to be used only in extreme cases.

Since virtually all developed societies in human history have been, essentially, totalitarian regimes, giving ordinary citizens the right of self-determination was a dramatic departure from the norm. For England to not change its treatment of the American colonies was being conservative. That would have been just business as usual for the empires of the world. For them to have modified their policies toward the colonies, granting more freedom to make for happier colonialists would have been being liberal.

Failure to become liberal meant that while the majority of colonists would have been appeased by liberal changes and remained English citizens, the enormous upheavals of the Revolutionary War allowed the creation of something far more radical than the vast majority of citizens were pushing for to begin with. By government's choosing to rigidly adhere to the conservative rather than moving to the liberal, the radicals ultimately won the day. Thus a radical concept, full rights for all citizens, won the day through radical action, open warfare. The fact that *"all men"* only applied to a select minority of all the adults living in the colonies shows the basic conservatism of the vast majority of citizens, even while being willing to be so radical as to fight a civil war for their freedom.

If a radical change is successful in taking control of a society, with the passage of time successive generations grow up adapting to the reality of the world they know and coming to support it. With enough time, that which was once dramatically radical comes to be supported by the vast majority and eventually is the conservative position, held by most citizens.

This happened in Russia, where totalitarian communism came to power in the '20s. Then at the end of World War II, the Soviet Union extended communist domination to a number of nations, including Czechoslovakia, Poland, Romania, Hungary, and East Germany. As the decades passed, the majority of citizens in these countries became patriotic supporters of their government, even though citizens of the West saw all these governments as brutally totalitarian. These conservatives strongly supported communism.

The spread of communism into China and then into Korea and Indochina, as radically brutal as it was, created governments where their citizens came to strongly support a communist one-party rule over their lives. The old radical became the new conservative.

Decades later, as the Soviet Union gradually began its slow decline and ultimate dismantling, Western ideas, diametrically opposed to the thinking of the majority of the citizens in communist countries in earlier times, began to be embraced with great enthusiasm as the ruling powers became more and more impotent. In an almost sudden rush, a number of nationalities suddenly had thrust upon them a dramatic choice. Since the communist governments they had long known and supported were coming to an end, citizens of each country had to work out a new design for government.

Several of these governments became representative democracies, embracing liberal thinking similar to that of the American colonies in the late 1700s. A number of others, while no longer officially being communist, nonetheless were taken over by strongman type governments similar to the communist rulers who had preceded them for decades. These nations essentially continued the same one party control, with the only substantive change being dropping the communist label.

The countries that successfully embraced Western ideas of representative government have by now no wish to return to the old conservative, Soviet style totalitarianism. The majority desire in these countries now that which these citizens want to conserve and protect is government of, by, and for the people. However, in those countries with modified Soviet style governments, there is still a great unrest, with some of them likely to become more liberal with time and others to morph into one form or another of totalitarian control.

As mentioned above, Russia itself, and some of the immediately adjacent nations, especially with large populations of Russians, is still divided between the liberals, who long for the freedoms enjoyed in the west, and the conservatives, who long for the glory days of the old Soviet Union. It may be a long time before true representative democracy replaces the way things used to be under communist rule.

An interesting development is that as communist governments gradually become more and more dysfunctional, a hybrid form of communism has spread in which, though the Communist Party, with or without that official name, continues political control, a market economy is allowed to flourish. Some aspects of capitalism appear, such as individual ownership of property and the allowing and even encouraging of entrepreneurial growth. After the end of the Soviet Union in 1991, most of the European former members of the Soviet Union immediately liberalized their governments and began to bring in Western political scientists and economists to help them begin to recover from decades of economic mismanagement that rendered these countries so noncompetitive in the international marketplace. The Baltic States and nations that were not members of the Soviet Union, but merely had communist governments imposed on them after the end of World War II (mostly Warsaw Pact countries), are primarily the ones who most quickly embraced Western-style democracy after the end of the Soviet Union.

Those communist countries that were closely allied to

communist China were much less affected by the fall of the Soviet Union and followed the pattern of China's rulers by gradually loosening the government's centralized control of the economies and allowing people's motivation and creativity to begin to revitalize their faltering economies. The general assumption, certainly the desire, in the West was that, once capitalism replaced communism in the economies, democracy would replace communism in the political. Whether and how this will happen will likely be one of the great dramas of the twenty-first century.

Careful management by the central governmental authorities has so far been able to continue to exercise political and military control, allowing very limited freedom of the press, religion, speech, or the ballot, while allowing radical new economic freedoms. This would have, in the old days of communist rule, been seen as treason. In so doing, these one-party governments have, in practice, gutted the core of communist orthodoxy.

These governments can even go so far as to rewrite parts, or all, of their constitutions and, in some cases, even remove the communist label while still embracing as much traditional communism as possible. It seems that most likely there will be a mixed bag of outcomes in these various experiments at having a nation composed of a totalitarian government with a capitalist economy.

CHAPTER ELEVEN

Today's — and Recent — Headlines

As of 2010, the only democratic government in a predominantly Muslim country was in Turkey, and it had a strong military control that would have been unacceptable in the West. The rest had governments of monarchs or dictators, secular or clerical, if there were strong central governments. Where central government had little power, governing was by tribes or warlords.

Thus, after years of growing tension, massive demonstrations broke out in Tunisia, resulting in the overthrow of the government of President Ben Ali, the dissolution of the secret police and the beginning of the process of establishing a more representative government. Emboldened by this example, mass protests broke out in Egypt, ultimately driving President Mubarak from power and beginning the process of building a new government.

Following these examples, protests began to pop up all across the Middle East. Libya was the next country to claim headlines around the world, as protests and government reactions quickly escalated into full-scale civil war. With the aid, this time, of NATO military intervention, the regime of Muammar Qaddafi was overthrown, leaving the nation with the highly unpredictable outcome in its efforts to establish a new type of government.

During this time, protests in Syria against the government of President al-Assad began to spread, with the regime giving a strong military response to the protesters. This gradually escalated into a full-scale civil war and, as this is being written (September 2012), the outcome is yet to be seen.

While there are commonalities among these nations involved in the Arab spring, there are significant differences in each country compared to the others. There have also been protests breaking out in most of the other countries in the Middle East, with some of the regimes seeming to have pretty good control over their people while others are very fragmented.

What is common to these movements is the desire of the majority of the people in each country to have the government replaced by new types of government that will be more pleasing to most of the people. With our Western history of replacing more authoritarian governments with governments which grant much more liberty to their citizens, it is enticing to think that these liberal movements will repeat our experience in the West. Just as the overthrow of the totalitarian Iraqi regime of Saddam Hussein has not led, after all these years, to the establishment of a functioning democracy and could well have endless years of bloodshed ahead before any fully functioning government is created, it will likely be a long time before we know which ones of all the governments in the region will actually become democratic, which ones will have a powerful majority which crushes minority rights, which ones will continue some form of secular dictatorship, and which ones will be ruled by Islamists, using their nations as launching pads for continuing violence against democratic governments.

While there currently is little US media attention given to sub-Saharan African nations that are experiencing a struggle between authoritarianism and liberty, for the distant future there will in all likelihood be nation after nation undergoing painful struggles and even civil wars as these nations sort out what type of governments they shall have for the future.

After decades of one of the most brutal military dictatorships, the country of Burma, also known as Myanmar, has in the last years allowed a rather radical liberalization of both its laws and the rights of former dissidents to begin to participate in the making of laws and the running of the government. This very recent attempt at a more open government, after so many decades of totalitarian inflexibility, suggests there may be many steps and missteps in the years ahead, before a fully functioning government of, by, and for the people can be established. It also remains to be seen how minority rights will be treated.

In the years following the fall of the Soviet Union, Russia and the United States began to share common cause on a variety of issues that raised a lot of hope of widespread future cooperation between Russia and the West, especially the United States. A real openness occurred for several years while Russia struggled with a huge variety of challenges as it attempted to begin to be a democracy. With the technical competence that had been developed during the twentieth century coupled with the vast land area controlled by Russia and its enormous mineral wealth, the future for Russia could be exceedingly bright, indeed. The last decade, however, seems to have put a huge dent in the upward trajectory of Russia as a potentially thriving democracy. The biggest question seems to be whether the former KGB agent, operating as a virtual dictator, intends to be the strong man who cleans up a society very much in need of cleaning up, and then lets the government truly begin to function as a healthy democracy, or whether he simply, like virtually all strongmen before him, intends to hold on to all the personal power he can for as long as he can, and let the nation suffer the consequences when he passes. In 1961, at the height of the Cold War, when we had great fear of the Russia-China Communist enemy, Baylor history professor Guy B. Harrison shared his belief that as history unfolded in the coming decades, the United States would wind up partnering with Russia to serve as a counterbalance to the growing global power of communist China. Putin definitely seems to be slowing down the likelihood of such a cooperation.

The biggest financial news of the last decade has been the enormous growth of the Chinese economy, resulting from the communist one-party controlling the government and the military while allowing economic freedoms dramatically at odds with communist orthodoxy. This growth is now being seen as having been gained at the costs of an enormous amount of corruption, dislocation of the population, widespread environmental damage, disfranchisement of people's rights by the growing aristocracy and many such problems typical of nations where there is no real government restraint to the power of the extremely rich and powerful. Much of the luster of the Chinese miracle has been tarnished by events unfolding in recent years. There is also a huge question how the new party elite now taking over the reins of power will govern differently from those who are retiring. Will China be able to correct these huge misdirections?

Will it be able to become and remain the largest global economy in the decades ahead? If so, will its people ultimately be able to establish a government of the people to replace the government of the communist elite? As they liberalize their production, will they continue to destroy their environment with their conservative approach to energy? And will the rapidly expanding Chinese military, therefore, be a military that answers to a government of by and for the people, or will it be a communist force used to intimidate Third World countries that are gradually developing into their futures and perhaps even to threaten Western democracies?

CHAPTER TWELVE

CHANGING TIMES — CHANGING MINDS

1. At the time of the American Revolution, democracy was usually seen as mob rule, only a step above anarchy. The fear was that the great mass of common people were not sufficiently educated or understanding of all the responsibilities of governing or that they could be too easily manipulated emotionally by demagogues. Even though government of, by, and for the people was a concept growing in popularity, all the governments anyone had experience with were governments run by the aristocracy. Even those who truly championed the concept of government of, by, and for the people, seemed to primarily mean educated, wealthy people. The idea of throwing open the gates of governmental power to the great unwashed masses was, apparently, simply too radical a concept for so many. Also this reaction to the idea of democracy was primarily concerning pure democracy, rather than representative democracy.

Since pure democracy proves far too unwieldy when dealing with millions of citizens, representative democracy became the style of government, specifically a republican style of government, in which representatives selected by the people actually run the government on a day-to-day basis. This also quiets one of the fears of a more pure democracy, the fear that a dangerously foolish vote could be taken in the heat of the moment, at a time of high emotion, and great harm could occur before it could be reversed. The republican form of government, especially with laws having to pass two legislative houses and even then being subject to a possible presidential veto, gives much more time to consider, more deliberately, the proposed solutions to pressing problems.

An additional safeguard built into our federal government is the separation of powers between the executive, the legislative and the judicial. However, even with the safeguards of a republican form of government and the separation of powers between the various branches of government, each time political power has been about to be extended to additional groups, the same alarm has been raised about the unpreparedness of the new group - women, blacks, 18 year-olds, etc - to wisely handle political power and the need to maintain the traditional ruling group to, alone, continue to decide what was best for the nation at large.

2. A successfully functioning democracy seems to require an educated, or at least literate, citizenry as a practical matter. Following from this, it also requires a free press, in order

for various ideas to be freely disseminated among the populace. In order for all citizens to be literate and preferably educated in general, free public education for all needs to come standard with democratic governments. Historically, totalitarian governments had a much more subservient populace if the people were left illiterate and ignorant. This severely limited the people's ability to think revolutionary thoughts and prevented the rise in power, for the people, that education brings.

It seems that totalitarian governments everywhere and in all times have thoroughly understood, and therefore feared, the critical truth that, "You shall know the truth, and the truth shall make you free." Such freedom for the masses is the last thing a totalitarian government wants. Allowing access to the truth is to them abysmally stupid.

Prior to the American Civil War, Southern states typically passed laws outlawing the education of slaves, fearing, no doubt correctly, that an educated slave population would pose a huge threat to the institution of slavery. In the century following the Civil War, leaving former slaves and their descendents illiterate, or at least uneducated, provided the ruling powers with the same two benefits of justifying keeping them disfranchised due to their lack of knowledge and preventing them from having the additional power that comes from being educated and using that power to succeed politically.

In the last two centuries, wherever totalitarian governments have continued to exist, rulers have found themselves doing a balancing act between keeping their citizens under subjection by limiting the flow of knowledge on the one hand, but on the other, needing to have their citizens knowledgeable in technical matters in order to have their nations be competitive with free nations. As much as possible, these governments want at least a certain portion of their populace to be educated in science and technology in order for the country to have the financial and military benefits for which such knowledge is essential. At the same time, they do everything within their power to prevent dissemination of liberal arts education, except as carefully crafted propaganda supporting the philosophies that justify the power of the rulers over the people. Coupled with this is the stifling of a free press, with all allowed news really being state propaganda.

The most glaring example of this, for decades in the twentieth century, was the Iron Curtain, the never-ending campaign by communist governments to keep their borders sealed to outside, democratic influences while continually bombarding their populace with the national party line. Being keenly aware of this, the West used its own broadcasts, such as Radio Free Europe, to, in some measure, defeat the communist governments' attempts to be the only sources of information and interpretation of events for their citizens. This remains the way things are still done all over the globe where free governments do not exist.

The latest information challenge to totalitarian governments is the Internet. This has made it necessary for these governments to exercise as extensive control as possible over their citizens' use of the Internet, attempting to filter out everything that doesn't support the government's party line. More specifically, social media has become a huge headache for these governments because of the power it gives ordinary citizens to communicate with each other in real time, to report what is happening in various areas, to upload pictures and videos and to, on short notice, call people together for mass demonstrations. It's hard to imagine the Arab spring having happened without the widespread use of social media. Of course, these governments can make use of the Internet, including social media, but at least there's more than one viewpoint being offered to the people at any given time.

3. Nations with a long history of liberal thought are in a much better position to establish successful representative democracies than are the nations lacking such an intellectual tradition, knowing only totalitarian governments prior to the attempt at real freedom. The poster child for this, of course, is the American Revolution, in which the 13 colonies successfully broke away from mother England and established a new nation, built upon the concept of government of, by and for the people (the concept, with the reality being quite a while in coming). This concept had been debated in Europe and the American colonies long before a physical revolution began.

The wide variety of intellectual positions, around this idea of self-governing, virtually guaranteed that no one political position was then or has since been able to rule the entire nation. Also the variety of religious traditions in the various colonies and the long history of open religious conflict in Europe ultimately lead to institutionalizing the concept of separation of church and state, thereby greatly reducing the likelihood of religious wars in the new nation. This experiment in creating a new type of government became the model that threatened business as usual elsewhere, first in Western Europe and later in other areas of the globe.

England could hardly escape being strongly influenced by the goings-on in its breakaway American colonies. Indeed, the American Revolution can be understood as simply one more chapter in a long history of liberal thought in England. The Magna Carta, even though it granted powers to the aristocracy rather than to the people, at least began to counterbalance the power of the monarchy and move the country toward the concept of power shared by many instead of the few.

France had a much more difficult time with its revolution. It had much the same intellectual ferment available among the educated as did England but had a monarchy that seemed to be even more detached from the realities of life among its commoners than was true for England. The French Revolution was a violent toppling of the monarchy, followed by various experiments in types of government, including a republic — Napoleon and a restoration of the monarchy, before anything resembling an effectively functioning democracy was established. One huge advantage the American colonies had in their revolution that the French did not was that the monarchy the colonies were fighting was separated by a large ocean. The French had no such luxury. And another was that though there were thirteen colonies, most citizens shared a common cause in throwing off the yoke of the British crown and parliament. And again, the French had no such luxury.

During the century and a half following the American Revolution, the rest of the nations in Western Europe, themselves having experienced for a couple of centuries the intellectual ferment challenging business as usual similar to that in America, England, and France, adopted representative governments to replace royal rule. The successful establishment of representative government was not accomplished quickly and easily in any of these countries. It only happened after a long history of intellectual ferment moving throughout the culture of Western Europe, rather like a farmer felling trees, clearing land, and plowing the field in preparation for deliberately growing the crops of his choice on his land.

A farmer cannot simply walk out into an overgrown forest, throw out a lot of seed, and expect that year to have a good harvest. A lot of work and time has to be put in well before any planting of a crop occurs. To not do the preparation work prior to sowing the seed pretty well guarantees a failed attempt at farming. Where nations have not had a long history of this type of intellectual ferment, the sowing of the seeds of democracy is a highly speculative enterprise.

There are a number of current illustrations of this reality. After the collapse of the Soviet Union, the countries that had had a long history of liberal thinking prior to being taken over by the Soviet Union at the end of World War II were the ones that have established strong democracies.

Those countries that technically gained their freedom from the Soviet Union but had limited liberal intellectual ferment and little history in employing concepts of representative government have generally either become shaky democracies with uncertain futures or have simply continued Soviet style dictatorships, without calling the country communist. The huge center of the old Soviet Union, Russia, seems still trapped in its long history of ironfisted czarist rule, ironfisted communist rule, and a continued attempted ironfisted rule by its current government.

China seemingly wants to be viewed, internationally, as a nation that represents the wishes of its people, but few citizens living in Western democracies would swap their governments for the Chinese style. The governments of sub-Saharan Africa either have never had anything close to an effectively functioning representative government or are currently experiencing political crises that threaten the future stability of these countries. The noncommunist governments of Asia, with a few exceptions such as South Korea and Japan, are still in the developmental stage of being truly democratic. And, as the daily news headlines continually remind us, the Arab spring shows no sign of being able to, in the foreseeable future, effectively deliver functioning government of, by, and for its people. These nations still seem most likely to continue their long histories of being one of three types of government: a strongman dictatorship, a strongman religious dictatorship, or a country of sectarian and tribal chaos.

4. A free society can lose its freedom to a totalitarian right-wing takeover or to a totalitarian left-wing takeover. Both groups are about power, and the more extreme a group is, the less willing it is to share its power with anyone who is not in total agreement with its ideological positions. Chapter 7 lists several examples of each. While those of us living in Western democracies can casually be satisfied that we have not had our rights taken away by either style of oligarchy, we would do well to remember that there have always been such groups working to establish their type of government with the power to crush dissent.

I have always found it troubling how right-wing populism seems to so readily grab support of large numbers of Americans, with so many people seemingly being unable to draw any parallels between the disastrous rise of right-wing governments in the past in other nations and similar trends unfolding locally.

I have also found it truly confusing how so many truly bright citizens have become enamored with communism, being seduced by the promises offered through the intellectual postures of Marxism while being so blind to the anti-freedom realities of all communist governments that already exist or have existed.

5. A very real danger for any people that attempts a revolutionary change of government is that the nation will descend into a long protracted civil war, with the citizens literally destroying their own nation by an unending internecine war of attrition.

The more the entire nation shares a general intellectual and cultural history, the less likelihood there seems to be of having such a horrid, sick outcome to the revolution. The American colonies had a much more limited civil war built into their revolution than might have been expected. Even the American Civil War, eighty-five years later, seems to have had a mercifully smaller number of atrocities performed citizen upon citizen than is likely to be the case in most of the nations currently experiencing the turmoil of regime change. In the Arab spring, the more homogeneous culture of Tunisia (aided, no doubt, by a history of allowing much more equality and education among its citizens, including its women) seems to have given it a huge boost toward regime change with a minimum of national disruption. The same has not been true of Egypt, and Libya was and is a disastrously more murderous affair. The patchwork societies of Iraq, Afghanistan, and Syria seem cursed to join in this future of civil strife and annihilation. It is yet to be seen what will be the futures of Lebanon, Jordan, and other similarly divided nations in the Middle East.

6. Any group that takes control of the government and can rule with little opposition will, in time, concentrate its power in the hands of the rulers and increasingly rob the people of their rights. Seemingly, power is far too intoxicating to humans for it to be a healthy thing, for individual people or for a society, for power to be concentrated in the hands of the few. The second intoxication that seems too addictive

to resist is the accumulation of wealth that is made possible by such power. Throughout human history, the rights and freedoms of individuals are again and again taken away by those who crave power and by greed.

In a study of Solomon's reign, Baylor professor Kyle Yates stated that there are few people who are really wise enough to be rich. He allowed that there are many who are clever enough, or have inherited enough, to be rich. The real challenge, however, is to be truly wise in the use of that wealth. He was pointing out that few have possessed such wisdom. Is it any different today?

Some system of democracy seems to be the best structure to, at least to some degree, put the brakes on our twin cravings for power and for wealth. As it is said, power corrupts and absolute power corrupts absolutely. It is equally true that wealth corrupts and absolute wealth corrupts absolutely.

Throughout history, however people have gained their wealth, they have defended its ownership as just and right and totally theirs. Whatever the economic and political structure, those on top essentially operated with the attitude "The system worked well for me and mine. What's wrong with you?"

After their fear of the return of the British, the founding fathers's biggest fear was the concentration of power in the hands of the few, coupled with a fear of inherited power. Their solution to this was to build a framework that would deliberately distribute power to a variety of people and agencies, hopefully with a counterbalancing effect preventing any one person or any groups from obtaining an inordinate amount of power.

The primary way of doing this was to establish a central government where those who held the reins of power had to be voted into office by the approval of their citizens. The second way was to structurally build in branches of government that had power specifically delegated to them while other powers were specifically delegated to other branches of government. Thus, we have separate legislative, administrative and judicial branches, each with specific powers that counterbalance the autonomy of the other branches.

The framers even split the legislative branch into two different branches, thereby preventing either from having exclusive power of making laws. A bicameral legislature spreads power wider than does a unicameral legislature. In our republican form of democracy, not only is the legislative branch elected by vote of the citizens but so too is the administrative branch as contrasted to the typical situation in parliamentary democracies where the prime minister or president, the administration, is selected by the legislators after their election.

Those documents and the early structures of government coming from those documents have proven amazingly durable and effective in guarding against those outcomes the founding statesmen so feared. Chief Justice John Marshall increased the power of the judiciary, further limiting the power of the legislative and executive branches. Various amendments over the years have further spread governmental power by giving the vote to classes of people who are initially excluded and by specifically limiting the term of the presidency.

During the 233 years of the United States federal government, forty-six presidents have served an average of just over five years each. Similarly, the heads of state of other modern western democracies have brief stays at the top.

Contrast that with the long tenure of heads of state in both the traditional right wing (typically king for life) as well as the twentieth century right-wing and left-wing governments. Fidel Castro ruled for forty-nine years; Kim Il-sung, forty-six; Muammar Gaddafi, forty-two; Francisco Franco, thirty-six; Mao Zedong, thirty-one; Hosni Mubarak, thirty; Hafez al-Assad, thirty; Joseph Stalin, twenty-nine; Ben Ali, twenty-four; Ho Chi Minh, twenty-four; and Benito Mussolini, twenty-one. Which one of these regimes would you choose over the government you currently have?

Apparently, one of the essential structural features — if a government is to guard against too much accumulation of power at the top and the seemingly inevitable increase in the abuse of power and pervasive corruption — is to build in, by rule and by practice, a frequent exodus of the chief executive from the most powerful office in the land, relinquishing it to another, chosen by some system of multiple votes. This means the office cannot be inherited. It seems that, with little exception, only first world countries come close to accomplishing this.

Each of us needs some power and some wealth in order to be effective in living life as a citizen, an employee, a spouse, or a parent. A society works optimally when all of us have an appropriate amount of both rather than a few having an enormous accumulation and the rest making do with leftovers.

In every form of government in history, there have been

people who were driven to seize as much power and as much wealth while excluding as much as possible all others. There will always be such people. A properly functioning democratic form of government seems to offer the best protection against such theft of power and theft of wealth.